Lights Out

Lights Out

60 sensational recipes for late night bites

Jenny White

MQP

Published by **MQ Publications Limited**
12 The Ivories, 6–8 Northampton Street
London N1 2HY
Tel: 44 (0)20 7359 2244
Fax: 44 (0)20 7359 1616
email: mail@mqpublications.com
website: www.mqpublications.com

Design and illustration: Jo Hill
Photography: Peartree Digital Photography
Home Economy: Jenny White

ISBN: 1-84072-795-0

1 3 5 7 9 0 8 6 4 2

Printed and bound in France by *Partenaires-Livres*® (JL)

This book contains the opinions and ideas of the author. It is intended to
provide helpful and informative material on the subjects addressed in
this book and is sold with the understanding that the author and
publisher are not engaged in rendering any kind of personal
professional services in this book. The author and publisher disclaim all
responsibility for any liability, loss, or risk, personal or otherwise, which
is incurred as a consequence, directly or indirectly, of the use and
application of any of the contents of this book.

Introduction

When the sun goes down and the lights go out, it's time to get in the kitchen and indulge those late-night cravings. Whether it's a cheeky temptation that you can linger over in bed, a hearty fix to sort out your raging hunger after a big night out, or a calming soporific to ease you into gentle dreams, this fun and frivolous book provides you with all the recipes you'll ever need.

Enjoy a big bowl of sticky maple syrup and cinnamon popcorn with your friends as you watch a late-night movie, or pass round plates of pizza squares, mini bruschetta and sticky barbecue ribs to really get a slumber party going. Sink your teeth into a juicy steak sandwich with Swiss cheese when you get in late, or take an enormous bowl of sticky toffee pudding to bed with you—and make sure you remember two spoons!

For those times when you're up in the night with munching on your mind, why not rustle up a French toast and fresh fig sandwich or tuck into a simple bowl of homemade granola. And finally, when you're ready to sleep, sip a steaming lemon and honey hot toddy or nibble a calming lavender cookie and feel yourself dozing off in minutes...

1

Party On

Sensational sleepovers

Maple Cinnamon Popcorn

Sweet and sticky maple-flavored popcorn spiced with warm cinnamon makes a perfect snack when you've got friends coming over to watch a movie. Make a big bowl, sit back, and start licking those fingers!

SERVES 6

2 tbsp/25g butter
1 cup/175g popping corn
2 tbsp brown sugar
4 tbsp maple syrup
1 tsp cinnamon

1 Select a large pan with a tight-fitting lid and melt the butter. Add the popping corn, cover the pan tightly, and heat over a medium heat until the corn has stopped popping. (Shake the pan once or twice before removing from the heat just to make sure all the corn has popped.)

2 Remove the pan from the heat, uncover, and sprinkle over the sugar, maple syrup, and cinnamon. Mix well then tip into a big bowl and serve.

Cook's Tip

For easy eating, roll sheets of colored paper into cones and fill with popcorn. These individual portions are great for kids, particularly if you're looking for a relaxing evening in with a movie.

Mini Bruschetta
with Pesto, Parmesan & Olives

These classic Italian appetizers are perfect party food and make the ideal snack to go with drinks. No one can resist the bitesized pieces of crispy toast topped with a tasty, fresh pesto.

SERVES 8

8 slices French stick
1 tbsp olive oil
3 tbsp fresh pesto sauce
16 pitted black olives
1oz/25g Parmesan cheese shavings
Small fresh basil leaves, to garnish

1 Preheat the oven to 375°F/190°C/Gas 5. Cut the slices of French stick in half and lay them on a baking sheet. Drizzle with the oil and bake for 10 minutes, or until golden, turning the toasts over halfway through cooking.

2 Spread a little pesto on to each piece of toasted French stick and top with an olive. Arrange the Parmesan shavings on top and garnish each bruschetta with one or two basil leaves before serving.

Cook's Tip

You can vary the toppings if you like. Why not use hummus in place of the pesto, and top with a strip of marinated red pepper, or use fiery tomato salsa in place of the pesto, and top each one with a juicy cooked shrimp.

Tortilla Dippers

with Rich Tomato Salsa

Soft flour tortillas are fabulous deep-fried and, served with a rich, tangy tomato dip, they make the ultimate party snack. The dippers make great scoops for scraping up every morsel of this luscious, moreish dip.

SERVES 8

2 soft flour tortillas
Sunflower oil, for deep-frying
Salt and freshly ground black pepper
For the salsa
2 tbsp olive oil
1 garlic clove, crushed
1 red chili, seeded and chopped
1 (14oz/400g) can chopped tomatoes
2 tbsp tomato paste
6 baby plum tomatoes, halved

1 To make the salsa, heat half the oil in a small pan and add the garlic and chili. Cook for 1 minute, then add the chopped tomatoes and tomato paste. Season and simmer for 15 minutes. Meanwhile, preheat the broiler and arrange the baby plum tomatoes, cut side up in a small roasting pan. Drizzle over the remaining oil and season. Grill for 5–10 minutes, until charred at the edges. Stir into the tomato sauce.

2 Tear each flour tortilla into about eight pieces. Heat the oil in a deep pan to 385°F/196°C. (Alternatively, test the temperature by dropping a cube of day-old bread into the hot oil; it should brown in 40 seconds.)

3 Carefully drop a few pieces of tortilla into the oil and fry for 1–2 minutes, or until crisp and golden. Using a slotted spoon, remove the crisp tortilla chips from the oil and drain on kitchen paper. Fry the remaining tortilla pieces, then serve with the tomato salsa.

Honey Mustard Wedges

Everyone loves these sticky potato wedges, and the easy-to-make sour cream dip is the ideal accompaniment. You just won't be able to stop dipping once you start.

SERVES 8

8 medium-sized potatoes
2 tbsp olive oil
2 tbsp clear honey
1 tbsp wholegrain mustard
For the dip
⅔ cup/125ml sour cream
1 tbsp chopped fresh chives
Salt and freshly ground black pepper

1 Preheat the oven to 375°F/190°C/Gas 5. Cut the potatoes into chunky wedges and place in a single layer in a roasting pan.

2 Mix together the olive oil, honey, and mustard, and brush the mixture all over the potatoes. Season with salt and pepper and roast for 30–35 minutes, or until tender and golden.

3 Meanwhile, make the sour cream dip. Mix the sour cream with the chives and some salt and pepper. Spoon into a small bowl and serve with the potato wedges as soon as they are ready.

Cheat's Pissaladière

This is an easy version of the delicious French tart, covered with sweet, buttery, golden onions and olives. It makes a sophisticated alternative to the classic party pizza, cut into squares and served hot or warm.

SERVES 8

2 tbsp olive oil
1 tbsp/15g butter
3 large onions, peeled and sliced
1 garlic clove, finely chopped
Small bunch fresh flat leaf parsley, roughly chopped
13oz/375g packet ready-rolled puff pastry, thawed if frozen
12 pitted black olives
Salt and freshly ground black pepper

1 Preheat the oven to 375°F/190°C/Gas 5. Heat the olive oil and butter in a large skillet and add the onions. Cook over a gentle heat for 10–15 minutes, stirring occasionally, until golden and tender.

2 Add the garlic to the pan and cook for about 2 minutes. Stir in the chopped parsley and season to taste with salt and ground black pepper.

3 Unroll the pastry on a baking sheet and score a border about ½in/1cm from the edges. Spread the onion mixture evenly over the pastry, just inside the border and scatter the olives on top. Bake for 25–30 minutes, or until the pastry is risen and golden. Allow to cool slightly, and then cut into squares and serve.

Prosciutto, Mascarpone & Baby Tomato Pizza

Ready-made pizza bases and tomato sauce are a great last-minute standby. And, with the addition of a few extra ingredients, you can whip up a tasty party pizza in no time.

SERVES 4

Half a 10oz/290g packet pizza base mix
2 tbsp olive oil
4 tbsp/¼ cup ready-made tomato sauce
   for pizza
3 slices prosciutto
¾ cup/175g Mascarpone cheese
6 baby tomatoes
Handful fresh arugula leaves
Salt and freshly ground black pepper

1 Preheat the oven to 400°F/200°C/Gas 6. Make up the pizza base mix, according to the instructions on the packet, then roll out and brush with a little of the olive oil and spread the tomato sauce over the top.

2 Cut each prosciutto slice into three pieces. Drop spoonfuls of the Mascarpone cheese on to the pizza and arrange the prosciutto and cherry tomatoes on top. Season with salt and pepper, and drizzle over the remaining olive oil.

3 Bake for 20–25 minutes until golden and bubbling, then remove from the oven and scatter over the arugula leaves. Cut into wedges to serve.

Mushroom & Thyme Pizza Squares

Little squares of pizza make a fun party nibble. You can vary the toppings to make a larger selection of pizza squares. Try adding marinated artichokes, strips of roasted red bell pepper, and basil in place of the mushrooms and thyme.

SERVES 6

Half a 10oz/290g packet pizza base mix
Half a ¼oz/15g packet dried porcini
   mushrooms
3 tbsp olive oil
3oz/75g chestnut mushrooms,
   thickly sliced
2oz/50g oyster mushrooms
1 garlic clove, chopped
1 tbsp fresh thyme leaves
4 tbsp/¼ cup ready-made tomato sauce
   for pizza
5oz/150g mozzarella cheese, thickly sliced
5 pitted black olives
Salt and freshly ground black pepper

1 Preheat the oven to 400°F/200°C/ Gas 6. Make up the pizza base mix according to the instructions on the packet and roll out. Soak the porcini mushrooms in boiling water for about 10 minutes, and then drain well.

2 Heat 2 tbsp of the oil in a skillet and add the chestnut mushrooms. Fry for 3 minutes, or until starting to turn golden, and then add the oyster mushrooms and drained porcini. Add the garlic and thyme leaves, and cook for a further 2 minutes, then set aside.

3 Roll out the pizza dough to a 9in/23cm square. Brush the dough with the rest of the oil, and then spread over the tomato sauce. Arrange the mushrooms and mozzarella on top, and scatter over the olives. Bake for 20–25 minutes, or until risen and golden. Cut into squares and serve hot or warm.

Sausage & Caramelized Onion Mini-wraps

These fabulous mini wraps are a modern take on the old party favorite—sausage rolls. If you like, you can serve them with a bowl of tomato ketchup, for dipping, or just enjoy them as they are.

SERVES 8

4 good quality pork sausages
1 large red onion, peeled and cut
   into wedges
2 flour tortillas
2 tbsp mayonnaise
1 tbsp wholegrain mustard
Handful fresh flat leaf parsley, chopped
Salt and freshly ground black pepper

1 Heat a non-stick skillet over a medium heat and fry the sausages for 8–10 minutes, turning occasionally, until browned and cooked through. Remove from the pan and keep warm.

2 Add the onion to the pan and fry for 7–10 minutes over a low heat, until tender and golden. Meanwhile, warm the flour tortillas in a low oven.

3 Spread the mayonnaise and mustard over the tortillas and sprinkle over the parsley. Season with salt and pepper, and place two sausages end to end on each tortilla. Scatter the onions over the top of the sausages.

4 Roll up the tortillas around the sausages and onions and cut each roll into four pieces. Secure each individual wrap with a toothpick, if necessary, and serve straight away.

Garlic Chili Shrimp

These fragrant, spicy shrimp take only minutes to prepare and are a perfect last-minute party nibble. Serve them while they're still warm, and offer chunks of bread to mop up the garlicky juices. Offer napkins too for wiping those messy fingers!

SERVES 8

16 large raw shrimp
2 tbsp olive oil
1 garlic clove, finely chopped
1 red chili, seeded and finely chopped
Fresh cilantro leaves and lemon wedges,
  to serve

1 Peel the shrimp, leaving the tail section intact. Heat the oil in a large skillet and add the garlic and chili. Fry gently for 1 minute, until the garlic starts to soften.

2 Add the shrimp to the pan and cook for 3–4 minutes, turning occasionally until the shrimp are pink and cooked through. Spoon on to a serving plate, garnish with fresh cilantro leaves, and serve.

Thai-style Crab Cakes

Everyone loves this spicy Thai appetizer and it makes the perfect finger food at a party. You can make the crab cakes ahead and warm them through in a low oven just before serving.

SERVES 8

⅔ cup/75g all-purpose flour
½ tsp baking powder
1 egg, beaten
Splash of Thai fish sauce
Squeeze of lime juice
Splash of sweet chili sauce
½ cup/150g cooked crabmeat
2 sprigs fresh cilantro, chopped
Vegetable oil, for shallow frying
Salt and freshly ground black pepper
Sweet chili sauce, to serve

1 Sift the flour and baking powder into a bowl and stir in the egg, fish sauce, lime juice, and chili sauce until the mixture is smooth. Stir in the crab and cilantro, and season with salt and pepper.

2 Heat a shallow layer of vegetable oil in a non-stick skillet. Stir 2–3 tbsp cold water into the crab mixture and drop small tablespoonfuls into the pan. Fry for 1–2 minutes on each side, until golden and cooked through. Remove with a metal spatula and drain on kitchen paper.

3 Continue cooking spoonfuls of the mixture in batches until it has all been used. Serve the crab cakes while they are still hot, with a small bowl of sweet chili sauce, for dipping.

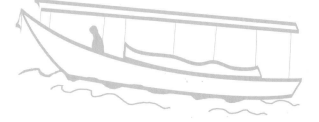

Chicken Satay Skewers
with Sweet Chili Sauce

**Always popular, this easy-to-make
version of the classic Indonesian snack
is wonderful served with a sweet chili
dip. It's great for a party because the
skewers mean your guests don't end up
with greasy fingers!**

SERVES 8

2 boneless, skinless chicken
   breast fillets
1 tbsp crunchy peanut butter
1 tbsp soy sauce
Pinch of hot chili powder
Sweet chili sauce, to serve

1 Soak 16 bamboo skewers in cold water
for at least 20 minutes. Cut each chicken
breast fillet lengthways into eight long
strips and thread each one on to a
skewer. Set aside.

2 Put the peanut butter in a small pan
with the soy sauce, chili powder and
⅓cup/80ml hot water. Stir over a gentle
heat, allowing the sauce to bubble until it
has thickened slightly.

3 Preheat the broiler to medium. Brush
the satay sauce all over the chicken
and place the skewers on a baking
sheet. Broil for 8–10 minutes, turning
occasionally, until the chicken is cooked
through. Serve hot or warm with sweet
chili dipping sauce.

Barbecue Ribs

in a Sweet & Sticky Sauce

You'll need to offer plenty of napkins with these gloriously sticky spare ribs —unless you want to watch all your friends getting into a right mess!

SERVES 8

3 tbsp all-purpose flour
2lb/900g pork spare ribs
2 tbsp dark soy sauce
2 tbsp tomato paste
4 tbsp clear honey
2 garlic cloves, finely chopped
Juice 1 orange
2 tsp English mustard

1 Preheat the broiler. Put the flour in a bowl, and season with salt and pepper. Add the ribs and toss to coat in the flour.

2 Mix the soy sauce, tomato paste, and honey in another bowl and stir in the garlic, orange juice, and mustard.

3 Shake any excess flour from the ribs and dip in the sauce. Place on a foil-lined broiling pan and broil for 20–30 minutes, turning frequently and basting with the remainder of the sauce until shiny and cooked right through.

2

Out on the Tiles

Big food after a big night out

Steak Sandwich
with Onions & Swiss Cheese

There's nothing like a chunky steak sandwich oozing melted cheese to finish off the evening. Use thin-cut frying steaks for this steak sandwich—they cook more quickly so you won't have to wait so long!

SERVES 2

1 ready-to-bake ciabatta bread
1 tbsp olive oil
1 small onion, sliced
2 tbsp chopped fresh parsley
2 thin-cut frying steaks,
   about 4oz/115g each
4 slices ready-sliced Swiss cheese
   (Emmenthal or Leerdammer)
Salt and freshly ground black pepper
Fresh flat leaf parsley, to garnish

1 Cook the ciabatta bread according to the instructions on the packet. Remove it from the oven and cut into two pieces, then cut each piece in half horizontally.

2 Heat the oil in a skillet, add the onion and cook for 4–5 minutes, or until tender and golden. Season with salt and pepper, and stir in the parsley. Spoon the onion mixture on to the bottom half of each piece of ciabatta.

3 Add the steaks to the pan and cook over a high heat for 2 minutes on each side, and then lay them on top of the onions. Top with the cheese slices, garnish with parsley, if liked, and finish with the remaining pieces of bread. Serve immediately.

Fish Finger Sandwiches
with Creamy Mayonnaise

A real winner, this one and the ultimate in speedy comfort food. If you prefer a bit of a sophisticated French twist, you can omit the ketchup and mayonnaise and add a couple of thin slices of Brie instead—delicious!

SERVES 2

8 fish fingers
4 slices white bread
Butter, for spreading
A little mayonnaise
A little tomato ketchup
Salt and freshly ground black pepper

1 Cook the fish fingers according to the instructions on the packet. Butter the slices of bread and spread two of them with a little mayonnaise and ketchup.

2 Place the cooked fish fingers on top of the mayonnaise and ketchup, and season with a little salt and pepper. Place the remaining slices of bread on top and serve straight away.

Zingy Hot Chicken Sandwiches with Capers

If you've got some leftover chicken in the refrigerator, this fabulous sandwich is the best way to dress it up. Tangy capers give it a real bite and contrast wonderfully with the deliciously creamy mayonnaise that squeezes out of the sides as you bite into the sandwich.

SERVES 2

4 crusty slices white bread
2 tbsp mayonnaise
1 tsp capers
1 ready-roasted chicken breast, sliced
Softened butter, for spreading
Salt and freshly ground black pepper

1 Toast the bread on one side until golden. In a small bowl, mix together the mayonnaise and capers, and then spread the mixture on the toasted side of two of the bread slices.

2 Arrange the chicken slices over the mayonnaise mixture and place the other two slices of bread, toasted side down, on top of the chicken.

3 Spread the top of the sandwich with some of the softened butter and broil until golden. Turn the sandwiches over, spread with butter, and broil as before. Cut each sandwich in half and serve hot.

Chorizo & Pea Tortilla

Fantastically satisfying, you can put almost anything you like in a tortilla —if you don't have any chorizo, use chunky ham instead. It's also delicious cold, so you could even make it before you go out!

SERVES 4-6

6 tbsp olive oil
1½lb/675g potatoes, thickly sliced
1 onion, chopped
8 eggs
4oz/115g chunk chorizo, chopped
1¼ cups/150g frozen peas
Salt and freshly ground black pepper

1 Heat 4 tbsp of the oil in a large, non-stick skillet and add the sliced potatoes. Cook over a gentle heat for 10–15 minutes, or until the potatoes are just tender and golden. Add the onion and cook for 5 minutes.

2 Meanwhile, beat the eggs in a large bowl and season with salt and pepper. Stir in the chorizo and peas, and then carefully tip in the potatoes and stir gently to just mix.

3 Heat the rest of the oil in the skillet and pour in the egg mixture. Cook gently for 8–10 minutes, or until the tortilla is almost set, and then place under a hot broiler for 5 minutes or so, until completely set. Serve hot, warm or cold, cut into wedges.

Spicy Chicken Kebabs

Nothing beats this tasty, healthy version of the classic kebab. It's pretty simple to make too so it won't be too much of a challenge after a late night out.

SERVES 4

4 skinless, boneless chicken breast fillets
2 tbsp olive oil
1 tbsp ground coriander
1 tbsp ground cumin
1 tsp ground turmeric
1 tsp chili powder
4 pita breads
4 handfuls shredded iceberg lettuce
2 tomatoes, sliced
1 small red onion, thinly sliced
Small handful fresh cilantro leaves
Salt and freshly ground black pepper
For the dressing
5½oz/150g pot natural yogurt
2 tbsp chopped fresh mint

1 Soak eight wooden skewers in water for 30 minutes. Cut the chicken breast fillets into large chunks and place in a bowl. Mix together the oil, ground coriander, cumin, turmeric, and chili powder, and season with salt and pepper. Pour over the chicken and mix well, then thread the chicken on to the skewers.

2 Heat a griddle pan until very hot and lay the skewers on it. Cook for about 10 minutes, turning the skewers occasionally, until the chicken is cooked through. Meanwhile, warm the pita breads in a low oven, then cut a slit along one side to make them into pockets.

3 To make the dressing, mix the yogurt and mint together, and season to taste.

4 Stuff the pita breads with lettuce, tomato, and sliced onion. Remove the cooked chicken from the skewers and pile into the pita breads. Drizzle with the dressing and serve.

Sausage Croissants

Tubes of ready-to-bake croissant dough are easy to find in the chiller section of most supermarkets and are just divine wrapped around chunky, piping-hot sausages. Vegetarian sausages will work just as well as traditional meat ones.

SERVES 4

8 good quality sausages
9oz/250g ready-to-bake croissant dough
1 egg, beaten
Mango chutney, to serve

1 Preheat the oven to 375°F/190°C/Gas 5. Put the sausages in a roasting pan and bake in the oven for 10 minutes, shaking the pan occasionally, until they have started to brown. Remove the sausages from the oven and turn up the oven to 425°F/220°C/Gas 7.

2 Unroll the croissant dough and cut it into eight strips. Wrap each sausage in a strip of croissant dough, leaving gaps so that the sausage is exposed.

3 Arrange the sausage croissants on baking sheets, spacing them slightly apart, and brush the dough with beaten egg. Bake for 10–15 minutes, or until the dough is risen and golden. Serve with a bowl of mango chutney, for dipping.

Spicy Omelet Wrap

It might sound like an unusual idea, but this omelet wrap stuffed with a spicy, tangy, melting filling is deliciously quick to make after a night out and just right when late-night hunger kicks in.

SERVES 1

1 tbsp olive oil
2 eggs, beaten
2 green onions, chopped
Pinch of dried chili flakes
1 soft flour tortilla
A little fruity brown sauce
1oz/25g mature Cheddar cheese, grated
Salt and freshly ground black pepper

1 Preheat the oven to 350°F/180°C/ Gas 4. Heat the oil in a small skillet (about the same size as the tortilla). Put the eggs in a bowl and stir in the green onions and chili flakes, and season with salt and pepper.

2 Pour the mixture into the skillet, swirling it around so that it covers the base of the pan and cook for 2–3 minutes, or until just set.

3 Meanwhile, wrap the flour tortilla in foil and warm in the oven for 5 minutes, and then spread it with a little brown sauce. Slide the cooked omelet on top and scatter with the grated cheese. Roll up and serve.

Easy Eggs Benedict

Traditionally served as a breakfast dish, Eggs Benedict is just as good late at night before you go to bed. Using ready-made Hollandaise sauce takes away all the hassle, and you'll be able to rustle up this feast in no time.

SERVES 2

2 large eggs
2 English muffins
2 slices good quality ham
2 tbsp ready-made Hollandaise sauce
Salt and freshly ground black pepper

1 Half-fill a small pan with water and bring it to the boil. Crack in the eggs and simmer gently for 2–3 minutes, or until the eggs are set. Meanwhile, toast the muffins on both sides, until golden.

2 Place the muffins on two serving plates and arrange a slice of ham on one half of each muffin. Remove the eggs with a slotted spoon and place one on top of each piece of ham.

3 Spoon the Hollandaise sauce over the egg and season with salt and pepper. Place the other muffin half on top, and serve straight away.

Melting Spicy Nachos

Often found on bar menus, nachos are fun to eat and tasty too. You can make them very easily and they're the perfect late-night bite—though once you start munching, you may find it hard to stop!

SERVES 2

4 good handfuls plain tortilla chips
1 large pickled chili, sliced
6oz/175g tub tomato salsa
2oz/50g Cheddar cheese, grated
2 tbsp sour cream
Fresh cilantro leaves, to garnish

1 Preheat the broiler. Pile the tortilla chips on an ovenproof serving plate and scatter over the pickled chili. Spoon over the tomato salsa in a fairly even layer and sprinkle over the cheese.

2 Place the nachos under the broiler for 3–4 minutes, or until the cheese has melted. Remove from the broiler and spoon on the sour cream. Garnish with cilantro leaves and serve.

Super-speedy Macaroni

Hearty and warming, this rich and stodgy feast is perfect if you've been out late on a cold winter's night.

SERVES 2

2 cups/225g quick-cook macaroni
½ cup/125g Mascarpone cheese
1 tsp English mustard
4oz/115g Gruyère cheese, grated
Salt and freshly ground black pepper

1 Cook the macaroni in a large pan of salted boiling water, according to the instructions on the packet.

2 Meanwhile, spoon the Mascarpone into a small pan with the mustard, and season with salt and ground black pepper. Heat gently, stirring, until melted, then bring the sauce to a simmer and stir in the grated Gruyère cheese.

3 Drain the macaroni well and fold into the cheese sauce. Spoon into big bowls and serve straight away.

> **Cook's Tip**
>
> If you've got time and want a crisp, golden top to your macaroni cheese, spoon into heatproof dishes, sprinkle a bit of extra cheese on top and finish it off under the broiler.

Quick Mushroom Carbonara

When you've got an urgent carb-craving, only a big, hearty bowl of pasta will do. Rich and creamy spaghetti carbonara is surprisingly quick and easy to make, and this one also has some mushrooms for extra flavor.

SERVES 4

12oz/350g spaghetti
⅔ cup/160ml heavy cream
1 garlic clove
⅓ cup/50g pancetta cubes
8 chestnut mushrooms, sliced
4 egg yolks, beaten
1oz/25g freshly grated Parmesan cheese
Salt and freshly ground black pepper

1 Cook the spaghetti in salted boiling water according to the instructions on the packet, until al dente. Drain well. Meanwhile, put the cream and garlic clove in a pan and bring to the boil. Set aside.

2 Heat a skillet, add the pancetta and mushrooms, and fry for 4–5 minutes, or until browned. Toss with the spaghetti.

3 Remove the garlic from the cream and pour over the spaghetti. Quickly stir in the egg yolks and Parmesan. Season to taste and serve immediately.

Spicy South-east Asian Peanut Chicken Noodles

Missed your dinner and went straight out? Whip up this warming feast when you get home, and you'll end the night feeling full and contented and ready for a good, long sleep.

SERVES 4

4oz/115g flat rice noodles
2 tbsp crunchy peanut butter
Pinch of hot chili powder
1 tbsp dark soy sauce
¾ cup/180ml carton coconut cream
½ cup/120ml hot water
2 ready-cooked chicken breast fillets, shredded
4 green onions, sliced
Small bunch fresh cilantro, roughly chopped

1 Cook the noodles in salted boiling water for 4 minutes, or until tender, and then drain well.

2 Meanwhile, put the peanut butter in a small pan with the chili powder, soy sauce, coconut cream, and hot water.

3 Stir over a gentle heat until combined, and add the chicken and green onions. Warm through for a few minutes, and then stir in the noodles and cilantro. Serve immediately.

Cook's Tip

Although this recipe calls for chicken breast fillets, if you happen to have any leftover cold roast chicken or pork in the refrigerator, these will work just as well.

3

Naughty Nibbles
Indulgent treats between the sheets

Tender Asparagus
with Herb & Garlic Butter

Juicy, melt-in-the-mouth asparagus with a deliciously herby, melted butter makes an extra-special treat to enjoy when you're just off to bed. Asparagus are at their best when they're in season, so make this a special treat to enjoy for those few months when they're at their most delicious.

SERVES 2

8 medium asparagus spears, trimmed
For the herb butter
¼ cup/50g butter, softened
1 garlic clove, very finely chopped
1 tbsp chopped mixed herbs, such as dill,
  parsley and basil
Salt and freshly ground black pepper

1 To make the herb butter, mix the softened butter with the garlic, herbs, and some salt and pepper.

2 Scoop the butter on to a sheet of plastic wrap and roll up, gently pressing into a sausage shape with your hands. Chill for about 30 minutes until firm.

3 Cook the asparagus in salted boiling water for 4–5 minutes, or until just tender. Drain well and pile on to a serving plate.

4 Slice the chilled butter thinly and arrange on top on the hot asparagus. Allow the butter to melt before serving.

Pears & Prosciutto
Drizzled with Honey

A very sophisticated late-night snack indeed! This is the perfect treat when you just need a little something to satisfy you before you turn in for the night. It's so light, that there's no risk of it keeping you awake either.

SERVES 2

1 ripe, juicy pear
2 slices prosciutto
1 tbsp orange-blossom clear honey

1 Cut the pear into quarters and remove the core, then cut each quarter in half.

2 Cut each slice of prosciutto into four pieces and wrap each piece around a wedge of pear. Drizzle each morsel with a little honey and serve.

Shrimp Tempura

with Spicy Dipping Sauce

If you're really pushing the boat out, these light, crispy tempura are really tasty—and perfect for feeding to your partner while you snuggle into bed.

SERVES 2

8 large raw shrimp
Sweet chili sauce, to serve
For the tempura batter
1 small egg
½ cup/125ml water
½ cup/55g all-purpose flour
Sunflower oil, for deep-frying

1 Carefully peel the shrimp, leaving the tail section intact.

2 To make the tempura batter, break the egg into a bowl and whisk in the water. Add the flour and whisk lightly; the mixture may look slightly lumpy, but don't worry—it'll be fine.

3 Pour enough oil for deep-frying into a deep-fat fryer or deep pan and heat to 370°F/188°C. Test by dropping a cube of day-old bread into the hot oil, it should brown in 60 seconds.

4 Dip the shrimp into the batter to coat, and then carefully lower them into the hot oil and fry until pale golden. Remove from the oil using a slotted spoon and drain on kitchen paper. Serve with a small bowl of sweet chili sauce, for dipping.

Creamy Salami Blinis

Ready-to-eat in minutes, these delicious mini pancakes topped with a twist of salami are very sophisticated and not too heavy to eat late at night.

SERVES 2

6 ready-made mini-pancakes
2 tbsp soured cream
2 tsp wholegrain mustard
3 slices salami
Basil leaves, to decorate (optional)
Salt and freshly ground black pepper

1 Arrange the mini pancakes on a serving plate. In a small bowl, mix together the sour cream and mustard and season with a little salt and pepper.

2 Cut each slice of salami in half. Spoon a little of the sour cream mixture on to each pancake and top with a twist of salami. Decorate with basil leaves, if liked, and serve immediately.

Cook's Tip

To make crab blinis, mix together ⅙cup/ 50g crabmeat, 2 tbsp mayonnaise, a squeeze lemon juice, and 2 tsp chopped fresh dill. Season with salt and pepper, then spoon the mixture on top of the pancakes, top with a sprig of dill, and serve immediately.

Hoisin Duck Pancakes

If you have a Chinese or Oriental supermarket near you, they often sell half ducks that have already been roasted, and these are perfect for making pancakes. However, this simple recipe using duck breasts offers a really great alternative.

SERVES 2

2 duck breasts
4 Chinese pancakes
4 tbsp hoisin sauce
2 large green onions, shredded
¼ cucumber, cut into matchsticks
Small handful fresh cilantro leaves
Salt and freshly ground black pepper

1 Preheat the oven to 375°F/190°C/Gas 5. Season the duck breasts with salt and pepper and place in a small roasting pan. Roast for 25–30 minutes, or until just cooked through. Remove from the oven and leave to rest for 5 minutes.

2 Wrap the Chinese pancakes in foil and place in the oven for a few minutes until warmed through.

3 Meanwhile, carefully remove the duck skin and discard. Slice the duck breasts thinly. Spread each pancake with hoisin sauce and arrange the duck, green onions, cucumber, and cilantro leaves on top. Roll up and eat straight away.

> **Cook's Tip**
>
> These pancake rolls can be messy to eat in bed, so make sure you take a pile of napkins to bed with you too!

Lemony Smoked Salmon & Cream Cheese Bagels

Another sensationally sophisticated snack to munch on in bed—smoked salmon, cream cheese, and lemon are a great combination. They're perfect first thing in the morning with a glass of orange juice, but even better last thing at night with a cheeky nightcap.

SERVES 2

2 plain bagels
4 tbsp cream cheese
Sprig fresh dill, finely chopped
Grated rind and juice ½ lemon
2oz/50g smoked salmon slices
Freshly ground black pepper
Lemon wedges, to serve

1 Using a serated knife, split the bagels in half horizontally. Mix together the cream cheese, dill, lemon rind, and juice and spread the mixture over one half of each bagel.

2 Fold the salmon slices over the cream cheese and season with plenty of black pepper. Place the other bagel halves on top and serve with extra lemon wedges for squeezing over.

Ice Cold Vanilla Cream Soda Floats

Ice cream floats are one of those often-forgotten treats of childhood that are just too good to forget about. So go on—indulge yourselves. There's nothing like cozying up under the duvet with this lip-lickingly, icy treat. Take a long-handled spoon too, to scrape up every last creamy, melting mouthful.

SERVES 2

2½ cups/600ml cream soda
2 scoops vanilla ice cream

1 Put two tall glasses in the freezer and chill for at least 30 minutes.

2 Pour the cream soda into the chilled glasses and drop a scoop of vanilla ice cream into each one. Serve with straws.

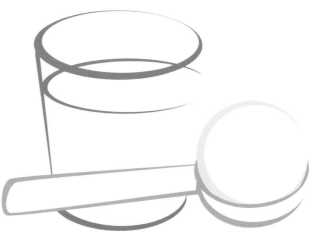

Super-quick Bailey's Chocolate Mousse

Wickedly dark and chocolatey and even more wicked to share, this is just the simplest, most decadent dessert imaginable! Make it in one bowl and take it to bed with two spoons for a really naughty night-time treat.

SERVES 2

2oz/50g bittersweet chocolate
½ cup/125g Mascarpone cheese
3 tbsp Bailey's Irish Cream liqueur

1 Break the chocolate into pieces and place in a heatproof bowl over a pan of gently simmering water. Stir occasionally until the chocolate has melted. Set aside for a few minutes to cool slightly.

2 Meanwhile, put the Mascarpone and Bailey's in a bowl and beat together until smooth and creamy. Stir in the cooled melted chocolate and chill for at least 30 minutes before serving.

Cook's Tip

To make a really indulgent Bailey's sundae, layer spoonfuls of the set mousse and scoops of chocolate and vanilla ice cream in a tall glass, then sprinkle chopped toasted nuts over the top and serve immediately.

Raspberry Ripple Shortbread Sandwiches

It doesn't have to be raspberry ripple —use any ice cream you like for these messy, naughty sandwiches. If you're feeling really wicked, you could even spoon over extra raspberry sauce to make a really super-sticky sandwich!

SERVES 2

4 round shortbread cookies
2 scoops raspberry ripple ice cream
Fresh berries and confectioners' sugar, to decorate (optional)

1 Place two of the shortbread cookies on a serving plate and place a scoop of raspberry ripple ice cream on top. Carefully balance the other shortbread cookies on top of the ice cream.

2 Pile fresh summer berries on top of the sandwiches, if liked, and dust with confectioners' sugar. Serve immediately and eat before the ice cream melts!

Chocolate and Banana Brioche Sandwiches

You just can't beat the combination of sticky chocolate and smooth, buttery banana. Slightly sweetened French brioche loaves are easy to find in most supermarkets and bakers. However, if you can't find brioche, you can use thickly sliced white bread instead.

SERVES 2

4 slices brioche
4 tbsp chocolate spread
2 small bananas

1 Take 2 of the brioche slices and spread 2 tbsp of the chocolate spread evenly over each one.

2 Peel the bananas, break into pieces and place in a bowl. Roughly mash with the back of a fork, then spoon the mixture on top of the chocolate spread.

3 Place the remaining brioche slices on top and pat down gently. Cut into triangles, if liked, and serve immediately.

Sticky Toffee Pudding

Not for the faint-hearted, this fabulously rich, sticky pudding is perfect for sharing and is always a winner. For a real treat, serve with extra cream poured over the top.

SERVES 2

¼ cup/50g butter, softened
¼ cup/50g brown sugar
1 egg, beaten
¾ cup/100g self-rising flour
Scant ¼ cup/55g chopped dates
2 tbsp milk
For the sauce
⅓ cup/75g brown sugar
½ cup/125ml heavy cream
¼ cup/50g butter

1 In a bowl, beat together the butter and sugar until light and fluffy, then beat in the egg a little at a time. Fold in the flour, then stir in the dates and enough of the milk to give the mixture a soft, dropping consistency.

2 Spoon the mixture into a buttered 4 cup/1¾ pint pudding bowl. Cut a round of waxed paper and a round of foil about 2in/5cm larger than the top of the bowl, and butter the bottom of the paper. Place both over the bowl and secure with string.

3 Put the bowl in a large pan and pour boiling water around the bowl, to come two-thirds of the way up the sides. Cover and simmer for 1–1½ hours until risen and springy when pressed. Check the water occasionally, topping up if necessary.

4 Put all the sauce ingredients in a small pan and heat gently, stirring, until combined. Simmer for 5 minutes, or until thickened. Turn the pudding out on to a plate and serve with the sauce.

Fruity Meringue Crush

Why have dessert after dinner when you could save it until bedtime? This light and simple late-night sweet snack is so easy to make and requires the minimum of preparation—with maximum, lip-licking pleasure!

SERVES 2

2 ready-made meringue nests
5½oz/150g strained plain yogurt
5 fresh strawberries, hulled and halved, plus extra to decorate

1 Roughly crush the meringue nests and reserve on a plate. Put the yogurt in a bowl and gently fold in the crushed meringue nests and strawberries.

2 Scatter a few extra strawberries on top to decorate and serve immediately with two spoons.

> **Cook's Tip**
>
> You can make this fabulous dessert using other fruits too. Try it with raspberries or sliced peaches in place of the strawberries, if you prefer.

4

Midnight Munchies

Fabulous feasts for after dark

Creamy Sage Polenta
with Melting Dolcelatte

If you're really hungry, this yummy treat is guaranteed to satisfy your appetite. There's nothing quite like creamy, golden polenta to fill you up and give you a feel-good glow.

SERVES 4

1½ cups/240g quick-cook polenta
2 tbsp/25g butter
12 fresh sage leaves, finely chopped
125g/4oz dolcelatte cheese
Salt and freshly ground black pepper

1 Bring 6 cups/1.5 liters salted water to the boil and add the polenta in a slow, steady stream, stirring continuously. Simmer for 1 minute, until thickened, then season to taste and stir in the butter and chopped sage leaves.

2 Divide the herby polenta among four bowls, crumble over the dolcelatte cheese, and serve immediately.

Mushrooms on Toast
with Fragrant Garlic

Tender, juicy mushrooms are delicious roasted with garlic and spooned over toast. The toast soaks up the tangy juices and tastes divine.

SERVES 2

4 large portabello mushrooms
1 small garlic clove, finely chopped
2 tbsp olive oil
2 thick slices country white bread
1 tbsp chopped fresh parsley
Salt and freshly ground black pepper

1 Preheat the oven to 375°F/190°C/Gas 5. Put the mushrooms in a small roasting pan and sprinkle the garlic over. Drizzle over the olive oil, season with salt and pepper, and bake for 15–20 minutes.

2 Toast the bread on both sides until golden. Place the toast on two serving plates and arrange the mushrooms on top. Pour over any juices from the pan, sprinkle over the parsley, and serve.

Cook's Tip

If you can't find portabello mushrooms, you can use ordinary mushrooms instead. Leave small ones whole, or slice larger ones into thick slices and pan-fry with the garlic until tender and juicy.

Best-ever Bacon Sandwich
with Sticky Maple Syrup

You just can't beat a bacon sandwich, and this one is even more tempting with its drizzle of maple syrup. The salty bacon and sweet, sticky syrup are a match made in heaven.

SERVES 2

4 strips thick cut smoked lean bacon
Softened butter, for spreading
4 thick slices white bread
2 tbsp tomato ketchup
2 tbsp maple syrup
Freshly ground black pepper

1 Preheat the broiler to high. Put the bacon on a broiling rack and broil for 2–3 minutes on each side, until crisp and golden brown.

2 Meanwhile, butter the bread, then spread with tomato ketchup. Lay 2 strips of bacon on 2 slices of the bread, and drizzle with the maple syrup.

3 Season with plenty of black pepper, and top with the remaining slices of bread. Pat down gently, cut in half, and serve immediately.

Pesto Scrambled Eggs
on Toasted Rye

Scrambled eggs are given a new twist with fresh pesto rippled through them. Chunky rye bread makes the perfect base for the aromatic basil-flavoured eggs, which are even better served with roasted baby tomatoes.

SERVES 2

Knob butter
4 eggs, lightly beaten
3 tbsp milk
2 tbsp fresh pesto sauce
4 slices rye bread
Salt and freshly ground black pepper

1 Melt the butter in a medium pan. Stir the eggs and milk together and pour the mixture into the pan. Stir continuously over a medium heat, until the eggs scramble and are cooked through.

2 Stir in the pesto and season the eggs to taste with salt and black pepper. Toast the rye bread on both sides until golden, and then arrange on two serving plates. Spoon the scrambled eggs on top and serve immediately.

Cook's Tip

Be careful not to overcook the eggs. Remove the pan from the heat while they're still moist because they'll carry on cooking for a while after you remove the pan from the heat.

Wholesome Peanut Toast
with Sweet Chili Sauce

Simple but delicious, you'll never think of peanut butter on toast in the same way again. Use chunky wholegrain bread if you have it as it really goes well with the nutty taste of the peanut butter and the spice of the sweet chilli sauce.

SERVES 1

2 chunky slices wholegrain bread
2 heaped tbsp crunchy peanut butter
Sweet chili sauce, for drizzling

1 Toast the bread on both sides until golden. Spread the peanut butter on to the toast, and then drizzle the sweet chili sauce over the top. Serve immediately while the toast is still warm and crisp.

Cinnamon & Raisin Bagels
with Chocolatey Cream Cheese

You can freeze split bagels, so they make a great standby for those late-night snack-emergencies! You can pop them straight into the toaster for a midnight bite and they're particularly good slathered with this rich, indulgent, creamy chocolate topping.

SERVES 4

3oz/75g bittersweet chocolate
7oz/200g tub soft cheese
4 raisin and cinnamon bagels

1 Break the chocolate into small pieces and place in a heatproof bowl. Place the bowl over a pan of simmering water and stir the chocolate occasionally, until melted. Remove the bowl from the pan and allow the chocolate to cool slightly.

2 Put the cheese in a bowl and stir in the melted chocolate. Split the bagels in half and toast the cut side until golden. Spread the chocolatey soft cheese over the bagels and serve.

Cook's Tip

A microwave will make quick work of melting the chocolate. Break the chocolate into a bowl as above, then heat in 30 second bursts, stirring between each burst, until melted.

Squidgy French Toast & Fresh Fig Sandwiches

Often known indulgently as 'eggy bread,' French toast is great for making deliciously soft hot sandwiches. Choose really ripe, soft figs with sweet pink flesh—ah delicious!

SERVES 2

3 eggs, beaten
4 thick slices white bread
1 tbsp/15g butter
1 tbsp superfine sugar
1 tsp ground cinnamon
4 fresh figs, sliced lengthways
Maple syrup or honey, for drizzling
  (optional)

1 Pour the beaten eggs into a shallow dish. Dip the slices of bread in the egg to coat them, allowing the excess to drip off.

2 Heat the butter in a large skillet and cook the eggy bread slices for about 2 minutes on each side, or until golden.

3 Meanwhile mix together the sugar and cinnamon in a small bowl and set aside.

4 Transfer the fried bread to a plate and sprinkle the cinnamon sugar mixture over each side. Arrange the fig slices on two pieces of bread and place the other two on top to make sandwiches. Serve immediately, drizzled with maple syrup or honey, if you like.

Cranberry Granola with Fresh Raspberries

Crunchy cereal is always a great quick-fix midnight feast, so why not make your own and have it ready for those times when you need it? And if you're not feeling peckish late at night, it's always fabulous first thing as a breakfast treat!

SERVES 6

2 cups/200g jumbo rolled oats
1 tbsp shredded coconut
⅓ cup/50g dried cranberries
½ tsp ground cinnamon
6 tbsp/75g butter, melted
⅓ cup/75g brown sugar
3 tbsp maple syrup
Milk or yogurt and fresh raspberries, to serve

1 Preheat the oven to 325°F/160°C/Gas 3. Toss all the ingredients together until thoroughly mixed, then spread the mixture out on a large baking sheet in an even layer. Bake for 35–40 minutes, or until golden and crunchy.

2 Remove the cereal from the oven and leave to cool. Break into clumps and serve in bowls with milk or yogurt and a handful of fresh raspberries.

Crumbly White Chocolate & Cherry Cookies

Make up a batch of these scrumptious cookies for those late-night moments when only something sweet will do. Just try not to eat them all at once as they're utterly irresistible!

MAKES 18

4oz/115g white chocolate
½ cup/115g sweet butter, softened
½ cup/125g superfine sugar
1 egg
1¼ cup/125g rolled oats
1¼ cups/150g all-purpose flour
½ tsp baking powder
½ cup/75g dried cherries

1 Preheat the oven to 350°F/180°C/Gas 4 and grease two baking sheets. Chop the white chocolate into small chunks and set aside. Cream the butter and sugar together in a bowl until pale and fluffy. Beat in the egg, and then add the oats.

2 Sift the flour and baking powder over the cookie mixture, and fold in. Stir in the white chocolate and cherries.

3 Drop dessertspoonfuls of the mixture on to the baking sheets, spacing them well apart. Flatten each one slightly and bake for 12–15 minutes, or until golden. Transfer to a wire rack to cool.

Dark Chocolate Brownies
with Pecan Nuts

Have a batch of these rich, sticky brownies ready for a midnight treat—served with a big scoop of ice cream. If you can keep your hands off them for long enough, they'll keep for several days in an airtight container.

MAKES 12

4oz/115g bittersweet chocolate
¾ cup/175g butter
2 cups/450g granulated sugar
3 eggs
1¾ cups/200g all-purpose flour
1½ tsp vanilla extract
1 cup/125g pecan nuts, chopped

1 Preheat the oven to 350°F/180°C/Gas 4. Butter a 13 × 9in/33 × 23cm non-stick baking pan. Break the bittersweet chocolate into pieces and place in a pan with the butter. Melt over a gentle heat, stirring occasionally, and then take the pan off the heat.

2 Add the sugar to the chocolate and stir until dissolved. Beat in the eggs, and then stir in the flour, vanilla extract, and pecan nuts. Pour the mixture into the pan and level the surface.

3 Bake for 20–25 minutes, or until the top of the brownies are shiny and set. Place the pan of brownies on a wire rack to cool, then cut into squares and serve.

Fried Bananas

with Rum & Brown Sugar

You won't be able to resist the rich, sticky sauce on these gooey, hot bananas. Serve with a dollop of whipped cream or ice cream for a comforting feast when you find yourself up in the night with a sugary craving.

SERVES 2

¼ cup/50g butter
2 bananas, peeled and halved
  lengthways
2 tbsp dark rum
2 tbsp brown sugar
whipped cream or ice cream,
  to serve

1 Melt the butter in a large skillet and add the bananas. Fry for 2 minutes on each side, until golden, and then add the rum and allow to bubble.

2 Sprinkle the brown sugar over the top, and reduce the heat, stirring the sauce around the bananas until the sugar has dissolved completely.

3 Increase the heat, and allow the sauce to bubble again for a minute or so, until the sauce is syrupy. Serve with whipped cream or ice cream.

Baked Peaches
with Honey & Ricotta

This is a great way of serving peaches that are not quite as ripe as they could be. They make a great midnight snack, but can also be served as a fabulously sophisticated dinner party dessert.

SERVES 2

2 ripe peaches
4 tbsp ricotta cheese
2 tbsp amaretto liqueur
2 tbsp clear honey
Redcurrants, to decorate (optional)

1 Preheat the oven to 400°F/200°C/ Gas 6. Halve the peaches and carefully lever out the pits using the point of a knife. Place the peaches cut side up in a small roasting pan and place a tablespoon of ricotta cheese in the center of each half.

2 In a small bowl, mix together the amaretto and honey and then drizzle the mixture over the peaches and ricotta.

3 Bake for 10–15 minutes, and then spoon into bowls and drizzle over any juices from the roasting pan. Serve hot, topped with a sprig of redcurrants.

5

And so to Bed

Soporific snacks for restful sleep

Calming Chamomile, Ginger & Honey Tea

Soothing chamomile is a natural calming remedy and the detoxifying properties of ginger are a perfect way to help you get to sleep. Sip this tea just before you turn in for the night, and feel yourself drifting off to sleep in minutes.

SERVES 1

3 slices peeled fresh root ginger
1 chamomile tea bag
2 tsp clear honey

1 Put the ginger into your favorite mug and fill almost to the top with boiling water. Allow to steep for 5 minutes, and then add the tea bag.

2 Steep for a further 2 minutes, then squeeze out the teabag and discard. Remove the ginger and discard that, too. Stir in the honey and drink.

Hot Milk with Fragrant, Warming Spices

Warm milk works every time if you're having trouble sleeping. Try this deliciously aromatic, spicy blend instead of the classic hot chocolate to help you relax, calm down, and enjoy a peaceful night's sleep. Zzzzzzzzzzz.

SERVES 4

2½ cups/600ml whole milk
1 tbsp brown sugar
1 cinnamon stick
4 cardamom pods, bruised
3 slices peeled fresh root ginger
Freshly grated nutmeg, to serve

1 Pour the milk into a pan and add the sugar, cinnamon stick, cardamom pods, and ginger. Bring almost to the boil, stirring constantly until the sugar has dissolved completely.

2 Remove from the heat, then leave to steep for 10 minutes. Strain the warm milk into heatproof glasses and sprinkle on a little grated nutmeg to serve.

Cook's Tip

If you don't want to use sugar for this delicious drink, you can use honey instead. Stir in about 2 tsp, then add a little more to taste.

Hot Chocolate with Cardamom & Whipped Cream

If you're in need of a comforting drink, this is the one for you. Warmed milk has been used as the classic bedtime soporific for centuries, and the soothing taste of chocolate and sweetly spiced cardamom are just delicious.

SERVES 2

2 cups/500ml whole milk
4 cardamom pods, bruised
4oz/115g bittersweet chocolate, chopped
½ cup/120ml heavy cream
Cocoa powder or shaved chocolate,
  to decorate (optional)

1 Pour the milk into a pan and add the cardamom pods. Bring almost to the boil, then remove from the heat and leave to steep for 10 minutes.

2 Remove the cardamom pods and return the pan to the heat. Heat gently, until almost boiling, and then whisk in the chocolate until melted. Pour into two large cups or mugs.

3 Whip the cream until it stands in very soft peaks, and spoon on top of the hot chocolate. Decorate with cocoa powder or shaved chocolate, if you like.

Lemon & Honey Hot Toddy

Stressed out or feeling a bit under the weather? Then a hot toddy will have you nodding off in no time! This classic winter warmer is the perfect bedtime tipple, and is particularly good for warding off the shivers.

SERVES 2

4 tbsp whisky
2 cinnamon sticks
Juice ½ lemon
2 tbsp clear honey

1 Divide the whisky between two heatproof glasses (preferably with handles), and add a cinnamon stick to each one.

2 Divide the lemon juice and honey between the glasses and top up with boiling water. Give each toddy a good stir with the cinnamon stick before serving.

Papaya & Ginger Yogurt

Pleasantly light and soothing, this healthy sweet snack is perfect before bed. Papaya is also said to aid the digestion, so if you've had a big dinner and it's making you restless, this might be just the thing to help you settle.

SERVES 2

1 small papaya
1 cup/240ml natural yogurt
1 piece stem ginger, finely chopped
2 tbsp syrup from the stem ginger jar

1 Peel the papaya, and then cut it in half and scoop out the seeds. Roughly chop the flesh and stir into the yogurt. Add the chopped stem ginger.

2 Divide between two serving bowls and drizzle with the stem ginger syrup.

Cook's Tip

Try making this dessert with fresh pineapple instead of papaya. Pineapple contains a similar digestion-aiding enzyme. Make sure it's fresh pineapple though, because the enzyme is destroyed when the fruit is canned.

Creamy Porridge
with Prune Compote

Porridge doesn't always have to be a breakfast dish—it's really comforting before you go to bed and will stop your tummy rumbling while you're asleep! Any kind of fruit compote or baked fruit goes well with porridge, so you can use other fruits instead of prunes if you like.

SERVES 4

1 cup/100g rolled oats
2½ cups/600ml milk
For the prune compote
12 ready-to-eat pitted prunes
½ cup/120ml Earl Grey tea
¼ cup/4 tbsp brown sugar
1 cinnamon stick
A little heavy cream, to serve

1 To make the prune compote, put the prunes in a small pan with the tea, sugar, and cinnamon stick. Stir over a gentle heat until the sugar has dissolved, and then bring to the boil. Reduce the heat and simmer for 3 minutes, or until syrupy. Remove from the heat and set aside.

2 Put the rolled oats and milk in a large pan and cook over a medium heat, stirring constantly, until the porridge thickens and comes to the boil. Simmer gently for 3 minutes, stirring, and then spoon into bowls.

3 Top each serving with generous spoonfuls of prune compote and a drizzle of heavy cream and serve immediately.

Rich Vanilla Muffins
with Banana and Raisins

Bought muffins aren't a patch on homemade—and they're so much better when they're still warm, fresh from the oven. These are simple to make and perfect for a late-night nibble.

MAKES 12

2¾ cups/300g all-purpose flour
2 tsp baking powder
½ cup/125g brown sugar
1 small banana, chopped
⅓ cup/50g raisins
1 egg
1 tsp vanilla extract
¾ cup/175ml milk
¼ cup/50g butter, melted

1 Preheat the oven to 400°F/200°C/ Gas 6. Line a 12-hole muffin pan with paper muffin cases. Sift the flour and baking powder together into a bowl, then stir in the sugar, banana, and raisins.

2 In a separate bowl, beat together the egg, vanilla, milk, and butter, and then stir this mixture into the dry ingredients until only just combined.

3 Spoon the mixture into the muffin cases and bake for 15–18 minutes, or until risen and just firm. Transfer the muffins to a wire rack and leave to cool.

> **Cook's Tip**
>
> For really light, tender results, be careful not to overmix the muffin mixture. Don't worry if the mixture still looks a bit lumpy—it'll be fine.

Fig & Honey Flapjacks

If you've got a batch of these sticky, chewy flapjacks ready, they won't stop you sleeping if you're hungry—just be sure to brush your teeth afterwards or you'll be in trouble with the dentist!

MAKES 14

1 cup/225g sweet butter
1 cup/225g superfine sugar
¼ cup/75g light corn syrup
⅓ cup/75g clear honey
4½ cups/450g rolled oats
⅓ cup/175g ready-to-eat dried figs, chopped

1 Preheat the oven to 350°F/180°C/Gas 4. Grease an 8 × 12in/20 × 30cm shallow baking pan and line the base and sides with waxed paper.

2 Put the butter, sugar, light corn syrup, and honey in a large pan and heat gently, stirring occasionally until the sugar has dissolved completely.

3 Remove the pan from the heat and stir in the rolled oats and figs. Spoon the mixture into the pan and spread out into the corners. Level the surface and bake for 20–25 minutes, or until golden.

4 Mark the hot flapjack into 14 bars, and then leave in the pan until cold. Turn out of the pan and cut into bars.

Lavender-scented Shortbread

A popular remedy in traditional medicine, lavender is said to help promote sleep. Try one of these fragrant shortbreads before going to bed and they should really do the trick.

MAKES 18–20

½ cup/125g superfine sugar
4 dried lavender flowers
1 cup/225g butter
2 cups/225g plain white flour
1 cup/120g ground rice
Pinch salt
Extra lavender flowers and superfine
  sugar, to decorate

1 Put the sugar and lavender in a food processor and whiz for about 10 seconds.

2 Cream together the butter and sugar until light and fluffy, then stir in the flour, ground rice and salt until the mixture resembles breadcrumbs.

3 Using your hands, gather the dough together and knead until it forms a ball. Roll into a sausage shape about 2in/5cm thick. Wrap in plastic wrap and chill for about 30 minutes, or until firm.

4 Preheat the oven to 375°F/190°C/Gas 5 and line two baking sheets with waxed paper. Slice the dough into ¼in/5mm rounds and place on the baking sheets. Gently push a lavender flower on to each biscuit and bake for 15–20 minutes, or until pale golden. Sprinkle with sugar and leave on the baking sheet for 10 minutes, then transfer to a wire rack to cool.

Marinated Red Bell Peppers with Basil

This light, aromatic snack won't keep you awake with a full stomach. Basil is used as a traditional calming remedy, so it should help you drift off to a peaceful slumber in no time at all.

SERVES 2

2 red bell peppers
1 garlic clove, unpeeled
2 tbsp olive oil
2 tsp balsamic vinegar
5 fresh basil leaves, roughly torn
Salt and freshly ground black pepper
Soda bread, to serve

1 Preheat the oven to 375°F/190°C/Gas 5. Put the bell peppers in a small roasting pan and roast for 20–30 minutes, turning occasionally until blackened. Add the garlic clove to the roasting pan for the last 10 minutes of cooking.

2 Take the bell peppers out of the pan, put them in a plastic bag and seal it. Leave until cool. Meanwhile, squeeze the garlic out of its skin into a small bowl. Whisk in the olive oil, balsamic vinegar, and basil, and season with salt and ground black pepper.

3 When the bell peppers are cool enough to handle, peel off their skins and remove any seeds. Slice the flesh and stir into the garlic mixture. Cover and set aside for 30 minutes–1 hour, before serving with soda bread.

Baby Jacket Potatoes
with Creamy Guacamole

Starchy potatoes always make you feel sleepy, and, with the addition of easily digested avocado, you should have no problems dozing off after this little late-night nibble.

SERVES 4

16 baby potatoes
2 tbsp olive oil
For the filling
1 large, ripe avocado
1 small garlic clove, finely chopped
Pinch dried chili flakes
Squeeze lime juice
Small bunch fresh cilantro, roughly
  chopped
Sea salt and freshly ground black pepper

1 Preheat the oven to 375°F/190°C/Gas 5. Rub the potatoes all over with the oil, and sprinkle with salt. Place in a roasting pan and cook for 25–35 minutes, or until tender when spiked with a sharp knife.

2 Meanwhile, halve, stone, and peel the avocado. Roughly chop the flesh and place in a bowl. Add the garlic, chili flakes, and lime juice, and mash together roughly with a fork. Stir in the cilantro.

3 To serve the potatoes, cut a cross in the top of each one, open out slightly, and spoon the guacamole into each one. Serve immediately.

Dreamy Lettuce & Pea Soup with Fried Bacon

Because lettuce contains great sleep-inducing chemicals, this is the perfect choice if you have to eat dinner late and you're worried about a full stomach keeping you awake. This soup is delicious and sustaining but lovely and calming too.

SERVES 4

2 tbsp/25g butter
2 strips smoked lean bacon, finely chopped
1 small onion, finely chopped
1 garlic clove, finely chopped
4 cups/1¾ pints chicken stock
2 little gem lettuces, shredded
½ cup/100g frozen peas
Small bunch fresh flat leaf parsley, roughly chopped
Salt and freshly ground black pepper

1 Heat the butter in a large pan and add the bacon. Fry for 1 minute, then add the onion and cook for 2–3 minutes, or until softened. Stir in the garlic and chicken stock and bring to a simmer.

2 Simmer uncovered for 10 minutes, then stir in the lettuce and peas. Season to taste with salt and pepper, and simmer for 3–4 minutes. Stir in the parsley, ladle into bowls and serve.

Weights and measures

The following conversions and equivalents will provide useful guidelines for international readers to follow. There's just one golden rule to remember when you're preparing your ingredients: always stay with one system of measurement—that way you'll achieve the best results from these recipes.

Liquid ingredients			Dry ingredients		
½ tsp	=	2.5ml	¼oz	=	10g
1 tsp	=	5ml	½oz	=	15g
1 tbsp.	=	15ml	³₄oz	=	20g
2 tbsp	=	30ml	1oz	=	25g
3 tbsp	=	45ml	1½oz	=	40g
¼ cup	=	60ml	2oz	=	50g
⅓ cup	=	80ml	2½oz	=	65g
½ cup	=	125ml	3oz	=	75g
⅔ cup	=	160ml	3½oz	=	90g
¾ cup	=	180ml	4oz	=	115g
1 cup	=	250ml	4½oz	=	130g
1½ cups	=	375ml	5oz	=	150g
2 cups	=	500ml	5½oz	=	165g
3 cups	=	750ml	6oz	=	175g
4 cups	=	1 liter	6½oz	=	185g
5 cups	=	1.2 liters	7oz	=	200g
6 cups	=	1.5 liters	7½oz	=	215g
8 cups	=	2 liters	8oz	=	225g

9oz	=	250g
10oz	=	275g
11oz	=	300g
12oz	=	350g
14oz	=	400g
15oz	=	425g
1lb	=	450g
1¼lb	=	500g
1½lb	=	675g
2lb	=	900g
2¼lb	=	1kg
3–3½lb	=	1.5kg
4–4½lb	=	1.75kg
5–5¼lb	=	2.25kg
6lb	=	2.75kg

Measurements

¼in	=	5mm
½in	=	1cm
¾in	=	2cm
1in	=	2.5cm
1½in	=	4cm
2in	=	5cm
2½in	=	6.5cm
3in	=	7.5cm
4in	=	10cm
5in	=	12.5cm

Glossary

The following glossary of culinary terms will provide useful guidelines for international readers to follow.

all-purpose flour: plain flour
arugula: rocket
baby tomatoes: cherry tomatoes
bell pepper: pepper
bittersweet chocolate: plain chocolate
broil: to grill
broiler: grill
cilantro: coriander
heavy cream: double cream
lean bacon: back bacon
light corn syrup: golden syrup
portabello mushrooms: field mushrooms
self-rising flour: self-raising flour
shredded coconut: desiccated coconut
skillet: frying pan
strained plain yogurt: Greek yogurt
strips: rashers
superfine sugar: caster sugar
sweet butter: unsalted butter
toothpick: cocktail stick
whole milk: full cream milk

Index